Greatest Positi
All t

VOL 1

"As soon as you trust yourself, you will know how to live." - Johann Wolfgang von

"Fear does not prevent death. It prevents life." - Naguib Mahfouz"

"It's OK to be scared. Being scared means you're about to do something really, really brave." — Mandy Hale

"You can, you should, and if you're brave enough to start, you will." - Stephen King

"The best is yet to be." - Robert Browning

"To forgive is to set a prisoner free and discover that the prisoner was you." - Lewis B. Smedes

"To the world, you may be one person, but to one person you are the world." — Dr. Seuss

HAPPINESS – CONFIDENCE – MOTIVATION - LOVE

Daniel Bulmez

DEDICATION

I dedicate this book to you, for blessing these pages with your beautiful gaze. For striving to achieve your dreams and become better than you are. I hope you achieve everything you desire and reach levels you never thought possible in all the areas important to you.

Life is a beautiful journey, and it is made that much more beautiful when we play, work, and grow together.

CONTENTS

Part 1: Confidence And Self-Belief

Quotes that encourage self-confidence and believing in one's abilities.

Part 2: Overcoming Fear

Quotes about facing fears and growing beyond comfort zones.

Part 3: Self-Motivation

Inspirational sayings to boost self-motivation and personal drive.

Part 1: Finding Joy In The Small Things

Quotes about appreciating life's little pleasures.

Part 2: Cultivating Happiness

Advice on building and maintaining happiness.

Part 3: Positivity In Daily Life

Encouraging phrases to remain positive every day.

Part 1: Fostering Relationships

Quotes on nurturing and valuing relationships.

Part 2: Love And Kindness

Sayings about spreading love and kindness to others.

Part 3: Forgiveness And Healing

Quotes on the power of forgiveness and moving past hurt.

Part 1: Being Present

Quotes about the importance of living in the moment.

Part 2: Meditation And Reflection

Sayings that encourage reflection and internal peace.

Part 3: Spiritual Wisdom

Quotes that offer spiritual insights and enlightenment.

ACKNOWLEDGMENTS

I would like to thank my Mother and Father for always believing in me.
Supporting me through the hardest times and with the little that they had.
Thank you for doing the best that you could and knew how.

I would like to thank my amazing friends from whom I learnt so very much. I
will always remember you for your support and for the things you may not
even know you have given me, by being such amazing people who I can look
up to and spend precious moments with.

You know who you are.

PREFACE

Introduction

Have you ever wondered how some people radiate positivity and attract success and happiness into their lives? How you too can cultivate a mindset that empowers you to achieve your greatest dreams and live a fulfilling life?

"The Greatest Positive Quotes of All Time" was specifically compiled to provide the wisdom and inspiration necessary to foster a positive mindset and overcome life's challenges. This collection draws from the greatest minds in history, offering insights to help you on your journey towards a happier, more successful life. It is here for you whenever you need a boost of positivity and motivation.

You can achieve a life filled with joy and success by embracing the wisdom in these powerful quotes. Use them to live a prosperous, happy, and fulfilling life.

I wish you boundless happiness and success as you embark on your journey. May these quotes inspire you to live your best life, on your own terms.

Good luck on your journey, and may all your dreams come true.

How to use this book

This book contains 7 chapters,each with 3 sections relevant to the chapter. Each Chapeter and section is designed to cultivate positivity and inspire success in various aspects of life.

Reading all the chapters in order will transform your perspective, providing you with the essential tools to nurture a positive mindset and achieve your goals. You may also refer to any chapter in any order. Choose whichever one is relevant to the challenges you are facing at that specific time, and let the wisdom within support you through it.

CHAPTER 1:

SELF-EMPOWERMENT

PART 1:

CONFIDENCE AND SELF-BELIEF

Quotes that encourage self-confidence and believing in one's abilities.

1. "Believe in yourself and all that you are. Know that there is something inside you that is greater than any obstacle." - Christian D. Larson

2. "Confidence is the most beautiful thing you can possess." - Sabrina Carpenter

3. "You are braver than you believe, stronger than you seem, and smarter than you think." - A.A. Milne

4. "With confidence, you have won before you have started." - Marcus Garvey

5. "To be yourself in a world that is constantly trying to make you something else is the greatest accomplishment." - Ralph Waldo Emerson

6. "Faith is having a positive attitude about what you can do and not worrying at all about what you can't do." - Joyce Meyer

7. "The most beautiful thing you can wear is confidence." - Blake Lively

8. "Believe you can and you're halfway there." - Theodore Roosevelt

9. "Confidence comes not from always being right but from not fearing to be wrong." - Peter T. McIntyre

10. "Argue for your limitations, and sure enough, they're yours." - Richard Bach

11. "Don't wait until everything is just right. It will never be perfect. There will always be challenges, obstacles, and less than perfect conditions. So what. Get started now." - Mark Victor Hansen

12. "Self-confidence is the memory of success." - David Storey

13. "Each time we face our fear, we gain strength, courage, and confidence in the doing." - Theodore Roosevelt

14. "The way to develop self-confidence is to do the thing you fear and get a record of successful experiences behind you." - William Jennings Bryan

15. "It is confidence in our bodies, minds, and spirits that allows us to keep looking for new adventures." - Oprah Winfrey

16. "Confidence is preparation. Everything else is beyond your control." - Richard Kline

17. "Confidence is contagious. So is lack of confidence." - Vince Lombardi

18. "You gain strength, courage, and confidence by every experience in which you really stop to look fear in the face." - Eleanor Roosevelt

19. "It's not who you are that holds you back, it's who you think you're not." - Denis Waitley

20. "Always remember you are braver than you believe, stronger than you seem, and smarter than you think." - Christopher Robin

21. "Act as if what you do makes a difference. It does." - William James

22. "If you hear a voice within you say 'you cannot paint,' then by all means paint, and that voice will be silenced." - Vincent Van Gogh

23. "Optimism is the faith that leads to achievement. Nothing can be done without hope and confidence." - Helen Keller

24. "The confidence which we have in ourselves gives birth to much of that which we have in others." - François de La Rochefoucauld

25. "Low self-confidence isn't a life sentence. Self-confidence can be learned, practiced, and mastered-just like any other skill. Once you master it, everything in your life will change for the better." - Barrie Davenport

26. "To love oneself is the beginning of a lifelong romance." - Oscar Wilde

27. "You wouldn't worry so much about what others think of you if you realized how seldom they do." - Eleanor Roosevelt

28. "Confidence is silent. Insecurities are loud." - Unknown

29. "Your success will be determined by your own confidence and fortitude." - Michelle Obama

30. "Only you can be the judge of your worth; and your goal is to discover infinite worth in yourself, no matter what anyone else thinks." - Deepak Chopra

31. "You are the only person on earth who can use your ability." - Zig Ziglar

32. "Confidence comes from hours and days and weeks and years of constant work and dedication." - Robert Staubach

33. "Don't wait until everything is just right. It will never be perfect. There will always be challenges, obstacles, and less-than-perfect conditions. So what. Get started now." - Mark Victor Hansen

34. "You yourself, as much as anybody in the entire universe, deserve your love and affection." - Buddha

35. "Trust yourself. You know more than you think you do." - Benjamin Spock

36. "Confidence is not 'they will like me'. Confidence is 'I'll be fine if they don't'." - Christina Grimmie

37. "You can have anything you want if you are willing to give up the belief that you can't have it." - Robert Anthony

38. "Always be yourself, express yourself, have faith in yourself, do not go out and look for a successful personality and duplicate it." - Bruce Lee

39. "One important key to success is self-confidence. An important key to self-confidence is preparation." - Arthur Ashe

40. "Low self-esteem is like driving through life with your hand-break on." - Maxwell Maltz

41. "You are more powerful than you know; you are beautiful just as you are." - Melissa Etheridge

42. "No one can make you feel inferior without your consent." - Eleanor Roosevelt

43. "If you have no confidence in self, you are twice defeated in the race of life." - Marcus Garvey

44. "Talk to yourself like you would to someone you love." - Brené Brown

45. "When you have confidence, you can have a lot of fun. And when you have fun, you can do amazing things." - Joe Namath

46. "As soon as you trust yourself, you will know how to live." - Johann Wolfgang von Goethe

47. "Self-belief does not necessarily ensure success, but self-disbelief assuredly spawns failure." - Albert Bandura

48. "Go confidently in the direction of your dreams. Live the life you have imagined." - Henry David Thoreau

49. "The more you believe in yourself, the more the world believes in you!" - Isa Zapata

PART 2:

OVERCOMING FEAR

Quotes about facing fears and growing beyond
comfort zones.

1. "The only thing we have to fear is fear itself." - Franklin D. Roosevelt

2. "Do one thing every day that scares you." - Eleanor Roosevelt

3. "Fear is only as deep as the mind allows." - Japanese Proverb

4. "I learned that courage was not the absence of fear, but the triumph over it. The brave man is not he who does not feel afraid, but he who conquers that fear." - Nelson Mandela

5. "Everything you've ever wanted is on the other side of fear." - George Addair

6. "Fear is a reaction. Courage is a decision." - Winston S. Churchill

7. "He who is not everyday conquering some fear has not learned the secret of life." - Ralph Waldo Emerson

8. "Fear is temporary. Regret is forever." - Unknown

9. "Avoiding danger is no safer in the long run than outright exposure. The fearful are caught as often as the bold." - Helen Keller

10. "Action cures fear, inaction creates terror." - Douglas Horton

11. "The brave may not live forever, but the cautious do not live at all." - Ashleigh Brilliant

12. "Expose yourself to your deepest fear; after that, fear has no power, and the fear of freedom shrinks and vanishes. You are free." - Jim Morrison

13. "What you resist persists." - Carl Jung

14. "The enemy is fear. We think it is hate; but, it is fear." - Gandhi

15. "Fear does not prevent death. It prevents life." - Naguib Mahfouz

16. "To escape fear, you have to go through it, not around." - Richie Norton

17. "It's OK to be scared. Being scared means you're about to do something really, really brave." - Mandy Hale

18. "There are very few monsters who warrant the fear we have of them." - André Gide

19. "The fear of facing your fears is harder to overcome than the fear itself." - Unknown

20. "There is no illusion greater than fear." - Lao Tzu

21. "Don't let the fear of striking out hold you back." - Babe Ruth

22. "Fear is nothing more than an obstacle that stands in the way of progress. In overcoming our fears, we can move forward stronger and wiser within ourselves." - Unknown

23. "Fear? If I have gained anything by damning myself, it is that I no longer have anything to fear." - Jean-Paul Sartre

24. "Inaction breeds doubt and fear. Action breeds confidence and courage. If you want to conquer fear, do not sit home and think about it. Go out and get busy." - Dale Carnegie

25. "Facing your fears robs them of their power." - Mark Burnett

26. "Our deepest fear is not that we are inadequate. Our deepest fear is that we are powerful beyond measure." - Marianne Williamson

27. "Fear kills more dreams than failure ever will." - Suzy Kassem

28. "Do not fear mistakes. You will know failure. Continue to reach out." - Benjamin Franklin

29. "Courage is not the absence of fear, but the triumph over it." - Nelson Mandela

30. "Everything you want is on the other side of fear." - Jack Canfield

31. "Fears are educated into us, and can, if we wish, be educated out." - Karl Augustus Menninger

32. "Feel the fear and do it anyway." - Susan Jeffers

33. "The cave you fear to enter holds the treasure you seek." - Joseph Campbell

34. "Too many of us are not living our dreams because we are living our fears." - Les Brown

35. "Don't let the fear of losing be greater than the excitement of winning." - Robert Kiyosaki

36. "Fear defeats more people than any other one thing in the world." - Ralph Waldo Emerson

37. "I am not afraid of storms, for I am learning how to sail my ship." - Louisa May Alcott

38. "Fear can keep us up all night long, but faith makes one fine pillow." - Philip Gulley

39. "Do the thing you fear and the death of fear is certain." - Ralph Waldo Emerson

40. "Fear is the path to the Dark Side. Fear leads to anger; anger leads to hate; hate leads to suffering." - Yoda

41. "You must do the thing you think you cannot do." - Eleanor Roosevelt

42. "Limits, like fear, are often just an illusion." - Michael Jordan

43. "The only way to get rid of the fear of doing something is to go out and do it." - Susan J. Jeffers

44. "Courage is resistance to fear, mastery of fear, not absence of fear." - Mark Twain

45. "Scared is what you're feeling. Brave is what you're doing." - Emma Donoghue

46. "Courage is being scared to death... and saddling up anyway." - John Wayne

47. "He who has overcome his fears will truly be free." - Aristotle

48. "If you are not willing to risk the unusual, you will have to settle for the ordinary." - Jim Rohn

49. "The fears we don't face become our limits." - Robin Sharma

PART 3:

SELF-MOTIVATION

Inspirational sayings to boost self-motivation and personal drive.

1. "The way to get started is to quit talking and begin doing." - Walt Disney

2. "Your limitation-it's only your imagination." - Unknown

3. "Push yourself, because no one else is going to do it for you." - Unknown

4. "Great things never come from comfort zones." - Neil Strauss

5. "Dream it. Wish it. Do it." - Unknown

6. "Success doesn't just find you. You have to go out and get it." - Unknown

7. "The harder you work for something, the greater you'll feel when you achieve it." - Unknown

8. "Dream bigger. Do bigger." - Unknown

9. "Don't stop when you're tired. Stop when you're done." - Unknown

10. "Wake up with determination. Go to bed with satisfaction." - Unknown

11. "Do something today that your future self will thank you for." - Sean Patrick Flanery

12. "Little things make big days." - Unknown

13. "It's going to be hard, but hard does not mean impossible." - Unknown

14. "Don't wait for opportunity. Create it." - Unknown

15. "Sometimes we're tested not to show our weaknesses, but to discover our strengths." - Unknown

16. "Motivation is what gets you started. Habit is what keeps you going." - Jim Ryun

17. "Keep your eyes on the stars, and your feet on the ground." - Theodore Roosevelt

18. "We aim above the mark to hit the mark." - Ralph Waldo Emerson

19. "One way to keep momentum going is to have constantly greater goals." - Michael Korda

20. "Change your life today. Don't gamble on the future, act now, without delay." - Simone de Beauvoir

21. "You don't have to be great to start, but you have to start to be great." - Zig Ziglar

22. "Set your goals high, and don't stop till you get there." - Bo Jackson

23. "Only the paranoid survive." - Andy Grove

24. "I find that the harder I work, the more luck I seem to have." - Thomas Jefferson

25. "Don't watch the clock; do what it does. Keep going." - Sam Levenson

26. "A river cuts through rock, not because of its power, but because of its persistence." - Jim Watkins

27. "You've got to get up every morning with determination if you're going to go to bed with satisfaction." - George Lorimer

28. "Start where you are. Use what you have. Do what you can." - Arthur Ashe

29. "The future depends on what you do today." - Mahatma Gandhi

30. "Be not afraid of going slowly, be afraid only of standing still." - Chinese Proverb

31. "You can't cross the sea merely by standing and staring at the water." - Rabindranath Tagore

32. "What you get by achieving your goals is not as important as what you become by achieving your goals." - Zig Ziglar

33. "The best time to plant a tree was 20 years ago. The second best time is now." - Chinese Proverb

34. "Either you run the day, or the day runs you." - Jim Rohn

35. "Whether you think you can or think you can't, you're right." - Henry Ford

36. "I am not a product of my circumstances. I am a product of my decisions." - Stephen Covey

37. "The only way to achieve the impossible is to believe it is possible." - Charles Kingsleigh

38. "You miss 100% of the shots you don't take." - Wayne Gretzky

39. "Motivation will almost always beat mere talent." - Norman Ralph Augustine

40. "Only put off until tomorrow what you are willing to die having left undone." - Pablo Picasso

41. "There is no traffic jam along the extra mile." - Roger Staubach

42. "You are your only limit." - Unknown

43. "Go as far as you can see; when you get there, you'll be able to see further." - Thomas Carlyle

44. "Never bend your head. Always hold it high. Look the world straight in the eye." - Helen Keller

45. "What you lack in talent can be made up with desire, hustle and giving 110% all the time." - Don Zimmer

46. "The only place where success comes before work is in the dictionary." - Vidal Sassoon

47. "Don't be afraid to give up the good to go for the great." - John D. Rockefeller

48. "If something is important enough, even if the odds are against you, you should still do it." - Elon Musk

49. "Do not wait to strike till the iron is hot; but make it hot by striking." - William Butler Yeats

50. "The man who moves a mountain begins by carrying away small stones." - Confucius

CHAPTER 2:

QUOTES ON HAPPINESS AND JOY

PART 1:

FINDING JOY IN THE SMALL THINGS

Quotes about appreciating life's little pleasures.

1. "Enjoy the little things, for one day you may look back and realize they were the big things." - Robert Brault

2. "It's the little details that are vital. Little things make big things happen." - John Wooden

3. "Life isn't a matter of milestones, but of moments." - Rose Kennedy

4. "Sometimes the smallest things take up the most room in your heart." - A.A. Milne

5. "Find ecstasy in life; the mere sense of living is joy enough." - Emily Dickinson

6. "There is joy to be found in every moment of living; each moment is a gift." - M.R. DeHaan

7. "Appreciate the little things, for they are the foundation of your life's happiness." - Unknown

8. "If you truly love nature, you will find beauty everywhere." - Vincent Van Gogh

9. "The art of being happy lies in the power of extracting happiness from common things." - Henry Ward Beecher

10. "Joy is not in things; it is in us." - Richard Wagner

11. "We tend to forget that happiness doesn't come as a result of getting something we don't have, but rather of recognizing and appreciating what we do have." - Frederick Keonig

12. "The small joys of life are the best joys of life." - Unknown

13. "Notice the small things. The rewards are inversely proportional." - Liz Vassey

14. "Be happy for this moment. This moment is your life." - Omar Khayyam

15. "It is the sweet, simple things of life which are the real ones after all." - Laura Ingalls Wilder

16. "Gratitude turns what we have into enough, and more." - Melody Beattie

17. "Joy comes in sips, not gulps." - Sharon Draper

18. "It's not how much we have, but how much we enjoy, that makes happiness." - Charles Spurgeon

19. "The little things? The little moments? They aren't little." - Jon Kabat-Zinn

20. "Sometimes it's the very people who no one imagines anything of who do the things no one can imagine." - Alan Turing

21. "Take joy in the small wonders every day brings." - Unknown

22. "Small things make base men proud." - William Shakespeare

23. "Do not spoil what you have by desiring what you have not; remember that what you now have was once among the things you only hoped for." - Epicurus

24. "Beauty can be seen in all things, seeing and composing the beauty is what separates the snapshot from the photograph." - Matt Hardy

25. "The best portion of your life will be the small, nameless moments you spend smiling with someone who matters to you." - Unknown

26. "Happiness is not a station you arrive at, but a manner of traveling." - Margaret Lee Runbeck

27. "Savor the simple and you enrich your life." - Unknown

28. "To find joy in the sky, the trees, the flowers... There are always flowers for those who want to see them." - Henri Matisse

29. "To see a world in a grain of sand and a heaven in a wild flower." - William Blake

30. "Let us be grateful to the people who make us happy; they are the charming gardeners who make our souls blossom." - Marcel Proust

31. "Every day may not be good, but there's something good in every day." - Alice Morse Earle

32. "Be mindful even if your mind is full." - James de la Vega

33. "The simple act of paying attention can take you a long way." - Keanu Reeves

34. "Joy is a net of love by which you can catch souls." - Mother Teresa

35. "Sometimes the little opportunities that fly at us each day can have the biggest impact." - Danny Wallace

36. "Celebrate the small things and our lives become bigger than ever." - Unknown

37. "Look closely. The beautiful may be small." - Immanuel Kant

38. "Joy is found not in finishing an activity but in doing it." - Greg Anderson

39. "Life is made up of small pleasures." - Norman Lear

40. "Find magic in the little things, and the big things you always expected will start to show up." - Isa Zapata

41. "The simple things are also the most extraordinary things, and only the wise can see them." - Paulo Coelho

42. "Beauty is everywhere. You only have to look to see it." - Bob Ross

43. "Each moment of the year has its own beauty, a picture which was never seen before, and which shall never be seen again." - Ralph Waldo Emerson

44. "A joyful heart is the normal result of a heart burning with love." - Mother Teresa

45. "We do not remember days, we remember moments." - Cesare Pavese

46. "Sometimes the best therapy is a long drive and music." - Unknown

47. "Life's most persistent and urgent question is, 'What are you doing for others?'" - Martin Luther King Jr.

48. "Learning to appreciate this beauty can change our lives." - Thich Nhat Hanh

49. "Life is about not knowing, having to change, taking the moment and making the best of it, without knowing what's going to happen next. Delicious ambiguity." - Gilda Radner

50. "Every small positive change we make in ourselves repays us in confidence in the future." - Alice Walker

51. "In order to carry a positive action we must develop here a positive vision." - Dalai Lama

52. "Give every day the chance to become the most beautiful of your life." - Mark Twain

53. "When you arise in the morning, think of what a precious privilege it is to be alive - to breathe, to think, to enjoy, to love." - Marcus Aurelius

54. "The simple act of paying positive attention to people has a great deal to do with productivity." - Tom Peters

55. "What you see depends mainly on what you look for." - John Lubbock

56. "Magic is believing in yourself, if you can do that, you can make anything happen." - Johann Wolfgang von Goethe

57. "Finding joy in the ordinary is not an ordinary thing." - Unknown

PART 2:

CULTIVATING
HAPPINESS

Advice on building and maintaining happiness.

1. "Happiness is not something ready-made. It comes from your own actions." - Dalai Lama

2. "The purpose of our lives is to be happy." - Dalai Lama

3. "For every minute you are angry you lose sixty seconds of happiness." - Ralph Waldo Emerson

4. "Happiness is when what you think, what you say, and what you do are in harmony." - Mahatma Gandhi

5. "Happiness is not a goal; it is a by-product." - Eleanor Roosevelt

6. "It is not how much we have, but how much we enjoy, that makes happiness." - Charles Spurgeon

7. "The greatest happiness you can have is knowing that you do not necessarily require happiness." - William Saroyan

8. "True happiness arises, in the first place, from the enjoyment of one's self." - Joseph Addison

9. "Happiness is a direction, not a place." - Sydney J. Harris

10. "Happiness depends upon ourselves." - Aristotle

11. "Happiness is not something you postpone for the future; it is something you design for the present." - Jim Rohn

12. "The only joy in the world is to begin." - Cesare Pavese

13. "Most folks are as happy as they make up their minds to be." - Abraham Lincoln

14. "Happiness often sneaks in through a door you didn't know you left open." - John Barrymore

15. "The secret of happiness is to find a congenial monotony." - V.S. Pritchett

16. "Happiness is not the absence of problems, it's the ability to deal with them." - Steve Maraboli

17. "Happiness is a state of activity." - Aristotle

18. "To be happy, we must not be too concerned with others." - Albert Camus

19. "If you want to be happy, be." - Leo Tolstoy

20. "Action may not always bring happiness, but there is no happiness without action." - William James

21. "Happiness is like a butterfly; the more you chase it, the more it will elude you, but if you

turn your attention to other things, it will come and sit softly on your shoulder." - Henry David Thoreau

22. "There is only one happiness in life, to love and be loved." - George Sand

23. "Happiness is not a matter of intensity but of balance and order and rhythm and harmony." - Thomas Merton

24. "People are just as happy as they make up their minds to be." - Abraham Lincoln

25. "The best way to cheer yourself up is to try to cheer somebody else up." - Mark Twain

26. "Time you enjoy wasting is not wasted time." - Marthe Troly-Curtin

27. "Happiness is the art of never holding in your mind the memory of any unpleasant thing that has passed." - Unknown

28. "To be without some of the things you want is an indispensable part of happiness." - Bertrand Russell

29. "Happiness is not having what you want. It is appreciating what you have." - Unknown

30. "True happiness is... to enjoy the present, without anxious dependence upon the future." - Lucius Annaeus Seneca

31. "Happiness doesn't result from what we get, but from what we give." - Ben Carson

32. "Happiness is a how; not a what. A talent, not an object." - Hermann Hesse

33. "The secret of happiness is freedom, the secret of freedom is courage." - Carrie Jones

34. "Happiness is the consequence of personal effort. You fight for it, strive for it, insist upon it, and sometimes even travel around the world looking for it." - Elizabeth Gilbert

35. "Happiness is always a choice. You can't wait for circumstances to get better. You have to create your own good fortune. So look for ways to be happy every day." - Joel Osteen

36. "Happiness is not a station you arrive at, but a manner of traveling." - Margaret Lee Runbeck

37. "Happiness cannot be traveled to, owned, earned, worn or consumed. Happiness is the spiritual experience of living every minute with love, grace, and gratitude." - Denis Waitley

38. "Happiness is not in the mere possession of money; it lies in the joy of achievement, in the

thrill of creative effort." - Franklin D. Roosevelt

39. "The joy of life comes from our encounters with new experiences, and hence there is no greater joy than to have an endlessly changing horizon, for each day to have a new and different sun." - Christopher McCandless

40. "Happiness is a perfume you cannot pour on others without getting some on yourself." - Ralph Waldo Emerson

41. "The foolish man seeks happiness in the distance, the wise grows it under his feet." - James Oppenheim

42. "You will never be happy if you continue to search for what happiness consists of. You will never live if you are looking for the meaning of life." - Albert Camus

43. "Happiness is the only good. The time to be happy is now. The place to be happy is here." - Robert G. Ingersoll

44. "If you want others to be happy, practice compassion. If you want to be happy, practice compassion." - Dalai Lama

45. "Happiness is something that comes into our lives through doors we don't even remember leaving open." - Rose Lane

46. "The best way to find out what we truly need is to get rid of what we don't." - Marie Kondo

47. "Three grand essentials to happiness in this life are something to do, something to love, and something to hope for." - Joseph Addison

48. "The true secret of happiness lies in the taking a genuine interest in all the details of daily life." - William Morris

49. "The happiness of your life depends on the quality of your thoughts." - Marcus Aurelius

50. "If you are too busy to laugh, you are too busy." - Proverb

51. "Happiness often sneaks in a door you did not think was open." - Unknown

52. "Happiness is not a state to arrive at, but a manner of traveling." - Margaret Lee Runbeck

53. "The only way to find true happiness is to risk being completely cut open." - Chuck Palahniuk

54. "Happiness is found in doing, not merely possessing." - Napoleon Hill

PART 3:

POSITIVITY IN DAILY LIFE

Encouraging phrases to remain positive every day.

1. "Keep your face to the sunshine and you cannot see a shadow." - Helen Keller

2. "Positive anything is better than negative nothing." - Elbert Hubbard

3. "Once you replace negative thoughts with positive ones, you'll start having positive results." - Willie Nelson

4. "The only time you fail is when you fall down and stay down." - Stephen Richards

5. "You cannot have a positive life and a negative mind." - Joyce Meyer

6. "When you think positive, good things happen." - Matt Kemp

7. "Live life to the fullest, and focus on the positive." - Matt Cameron

8. "Be the reason someone smiles today." - Unknown

9. "Choose to be optimistic, it feels better." - Dalai Lama

10. "Positivity always wins…Always." - Gary Vaynerchuk

11. "Positive thinking will let you do everything better than negative thinking will." - Zig Ziglar

12. "Surround yourself with positive people and you'll be a positive person." - Kellie Pickler

13. "A positive mindset brings positive things." - Philipp Reiter

14. "Be positive. Be true. Be kind." - Roy T. Bennett

15. "Vibrate good energy into others' soul, making them never forget the beauty of yours." - Unknown

16. "Positivity is a choice that becomes a lifestyle." - Unknown

17. "Positive thinking is more than just a tagline. It changes the way we behave." - Harvey Mackay

18. "Accentuate the positive, eliminate the negative, latch onto the affirmative." - Johnny Mercer

19. "A strong, positive self-image is the best possible preparation for success." - Joyce Brothers

20. "It's a wonderful thing to be optimistic. It keeps you healthy and it keeps you resilient." - Daniel Kahneman

21. "Find a place inside where there's joy, and the joy will burn out the pain." - Joseph Campbell

22. "The more you feed your mind with positive thoughts, the more you can attract great things into your life." - Roy T. Bennett

23. "Your positivity can become a castle around you which will protect you from the arrow of negativity." - Gurudev Shree Chitrabhanu

24. "Every day brings new choices." - Martha Beck

25. "Wherever you go, no matter what the weather, always bring your own sunshine." - Anthony J. D'Angelo

26. "Pessimism leads to weakness, optimism to power." - William James

27. "The positivity in our life is a function of our thinking. So think positive, stay positive!" - Unknown

28. "Adopting the right attitude can convert a negative stress into a positive one." - Hans Selye

29. "Optimism is a happiness magnet. If you stay positive, good things and good people will be drawn to you." - Mary Lou Retton

30. "Be mindful. Be grateful. Be positive. Be true. Be kind." - Roy T. Bennett

31. "What is the difference between an obstacle and an opportunity? Our attitude toward it. Every opportunity has a difficulty, and every difficulty has an opportunity." - J. Sidlow Baxter

32. "The less you respond to negative people, the more positive your life will become." - Paulo Coelho

33. "If you are positive, you'll see opportunities instead of obstacles." - Widad Akrawi

34. "Always turn a negative situation into a positive situation." - Michael Jordan

35. "When you are enthusiastic about what you do, you feel this positive energy. It's very simple." - Paulo Coelho

36. "Positive thoughts lead to positive results." - Maria V. Snyder

37. "You can, you should, and if you're brave enough to start, you will." - Stephen King

38. "Worry less, smile more. Don't regret, just learn and grow." - Unknown

39. "The only place where your dream becomes impossible is in your own thinking." - Robert H Schuller

40. "Things turn out best for the people who make the best of the way things turn out." - John Wooden

41. "I am too positive to be doubtful, too optimistic to be fearful, and too determined to be defeated." - Hussein Nishah

42. "Positive thinking is empowering; positive action is achieving." - Dr. T.P.Chia

43. "If you can stay positive in a negative situation, you win." - Unknown

44. "Keep a positive outlook even when faced with life challenges." - Catherine Pulsifer

45. "Believe that life is worth living and your belief will help create the fact." - William James

46. "Positivity helps with everything in life." - Lexi Thompson

47. "Think big thoughts but relish small pleasures." - H. Jackson Brown Jr.

48. "When things go wrong, don't go with them." - Elvis Presley

49. "Instead of worrying about what you cannot control, shift your energy to what you can create." - Roy T. Bennett

50. "A positive attitude causes a chain reaction of positive thoughts, events, and outcomes. It is a catalyst and it sparks extraordinary results." - Wade Boggs

51. "You always pass failure on the way to success." - Mickey Rooney

52. "The best is yet to be." - Robert Browning

53. "Do good and good will come to you." - Unknown

54. "The greatest discovery of any generation is that a human can alter his life by altering his attitude." - William James

55. "Your smile will give you a positive countenance that will make people feel comfortable around you." - Les Brown

56. "A positive attitude may not solve all your problems, but it will annoy enough people to make it worth the effort." - Herm Albright

57. "Train your mind to see the good in every situation." - Unknown

CHAPTER 3:

LOVE AND RELATIONSHIPS

PART 1:

FOSTERING RELATIONSHIPS

Quotes on nurturing and valuing relationships.

1. The most important thing in communication is hearing what isn't said." - Peter Drucker

2. "Treasure your relationships, not your possessions." - Anthony J. D'Angelo

3. "Relationships are the flavor of life." - Pawan Mishra

4. "The greatest gift of life is friendship, and I have received it." - Hubert H. Humphrey

5. "Assumptions are the termites of relationships." - Henry Winkler

6. "We are born of love; love is our mother." - Rumi

7. "A real friend is one who walks in when the rest of the world walks out." - Walter Winchell

8. "Personal relationships are the fertile soil from which all advancement, all success, all achievement in real life grows." - Ben Stein

9. "You don't develop courage by being happy in your relationships every day. You develop it by surviving difficult times and challenging adversity." - Epicurus

10. "Having someone wonder where you are when you don't come home at night is a very old human need." - Margaret Mead

11. "Be genuinely interested in everyone you meet and everyone you meet will be genuinely interested in you." - Rasheed Ogunlaru

12. "Each friend represents a world in us, a world possibly not born until they arrive." - Anaïs Nin

13. "Soul connections are not often found and are worth every bit of fight left in you to keep." - Shannon L. Alder

14. "What do we live for, if it is not to make life less difficult for each other?" - George Eliot

15. "The relationship between husband and wife should be one of closest friends." - B. R. Ambedkar

16. "No road is long with good company." - Turkish Proverb

17. "Shared joy is a double joy; shared sorrow is half a sorrow." - Swedish Proverb

18. "They may forget what you said, but they will never forget how you made them feel." - Carl W. Buechner

19. "For beautiful eyes, look for the good in others; for beautiful lips, speak only words of kindness; and for poise, walk with the knowledge that you are never alone." - Audrey Hepburn

20. "Don't walk behind me; I may not lead. Don't walk in front of me; I may not follow. Just walk beside me and be my friend." - Albert Camus

21. "The bond that links your true family is not one of blood, but of respect and joy in each other's life." - Richard Bach

22. "Relationships end too soon because people stop putting the same effort to keep you as they did to win you." - Unknown

23. "The best and most beautiful things in this world cannot be seen or even heard, but must be felt with the heart." - Helen Keller

24. "True friendships are eternal." - Cicero

25. "Ultimately the bond of all companionship, whether in marriage or in friendship, is conversation." - Oscar Wilde

26. "It is not a lack of love, but a lack of friendship that makes unhappy marriages." - Friedrich Nietzsche

27. "Every person is a new door to a different world." - Six Degrees of Separation

28. "We can improve our relationships with others by leaps and bounds if we become encouragers instead of critics." - Joyce Meyer

29. "It's not so much our friends' help that helps us, as the confidence of their help." - Epicurus

30. "You can make more friends in two months by becoming interested in other people than you can in two years by trying to get other people interested in you." - Dale Carnegie

31. "A loving relationship is one in which the loved one is free to be himself - to laugh with me, but never at me; to cry with me, but never because of me; to love life, to love himself, to love being loved." - Leo F. Buscaglia

32. "The only way to have a friend is to be one." - Ralph Waldo Emerson

33. "The best mirror is an old friend." - George Herbert

34. "In the sweetness of friendship let there be laughter and sharing of pleasures." - Khalil Gibran

35. "Friendship is born at that moment when one person says to another, 'What! You too? I thought I was the only one.'" - C.S. Lewis

36. "Let us be grateful to people who make us happy, they are the charming gardeners who make our souls blossom." - Marcel Proust

37. "A friend is someone who gives you total freedom to be yourself." - Jim Morrison

38. "Friends are those rare people who ask how we are and then wait to hear the answer." - Ed Cunningham

39. "Some people arrive and make such a beautiful impact on your life, you can barely remember what life was like without them." - Anna Taylor

40. "The most important thing in life is to learn how to give out love, and to let it come in." - Morrie Schwartz

41. "The greatest healing therapy is friendship and love." - Hubert H. Humphrey

42. "Relationships include: fights, jealousy, arguments, faith, tears, disagreements, but a real relationship fights through all that with love." - Unknown

43. "Any relationship requires attention and work and that investments always pays off." - Michelle Obama

44. "I like to listen. I have learned a great deal from listening carefully. Most people never listen." - Ernest Hemingway

45. "Every relationship needs an argument every now and then. Just to prove that it is strong enough to survive. Long-term relationships, the ones that matter, are all about weathering the peaks and the valleys." - Nicholas Sparks

46. "Surround yourself with only people who are going to lift you higher." - Oprah Winfrey

47. "Love is when the other person's happiness is more important than your own." - H. Jackson Brown Jr.

48. "We are most alive when we're in love." - John Updike

49. "It's not about having a perfect relationship, it's about finding someone who matches you and will go through everything without giving up." - Unknown

50. "Find a group of people who challenge and inspire you; spend a lot of time with them, and it will change your life." - Amy Poehler

51. "The best thing to hold onto in life is each other." - Audrey Hepburn

52. "Love one another and you will be happy. It's as simple and as difficult as that." - Michael Leunig

53. "To the world, you may be one person, but to one person you are the world." - Dr. Seuss

54. "A single rose can be my garden... a single friend, my world." - Leo Buscaglia

55. "Friendship is unnecessary, like philosophy, like art... It has no survival value; rather it is one of those things that give value to survival." - C.S. Lewis

56. "People are lonely because they build walls instead of bridges." - Joseph F. Newton Men

57. "An invisible thread connects those who are destined to meet, regardless of time, place, and circumstance. The thread may stretch or tangle, but it will never break." - Ancient Chinese Proverb

58. "Friendship improves happiness and abates misery, by the doubling of our joy and the dividing of our grief." - Marcus Tullius Cicero

PART 2:

LOVE AND KINDNESS

Sayings about spreading love and kindness to others.

1. Kindness in words creates confidence. Kindness in thinking creates profoundness. Kindness in giving creates love." - Lao Tzu

2. "Spread love everywhere you go. Let no one ever come to you without leaving happier." - Mother Teresa

3. "Where there is love there is life." - Mahatma Gandhi

4. "A single act of kindness throws out roots in all directions, and the roots spring up and make new trees." - Amelia Earhart

5. "Love and kindness are never wasted. They always make a difference." - Barbara De Angelis

6. "The only thing we never get enough of is love; and the only thing we never give enough of is love." - Henry Miller

7. "Love is not only something you feel, it is something you do." - David Wilkerson

8. "Kindness is the language which the deaf can hear and the blind can see." - Mark Twain

9. "I have decided to stick with love. Hate is too great a burden to bear." - Martin Luther King Jr.

10. "What wisdom can you find that is greater than kindness?" - Jean-Jacques Rousseau

11. "You can give without loving, but you cannot love without giving." - Amy Carmichael

12. "Be kind, for everyone you meet is fighting a harder battle." - Plato

13. "Let us always meet each other with smile, for the smile is the beginning of love." - Mother Teresa

14. "Kindness is a passport that opens doors and fashions friends. It softens hearts and molds relationships that can last lifetimes." - Joseph B. Wirthlin

15. "Do all things with love." - Og Mandino

16. "Carry out a random act of kindness, with no expectation of reward, safe in the knowledge that one day someone might do the same for you." - Princess Diana

17. "To love and be loved is to feel the sun from both sides." - David Viscott

18. "Too often we underestimate the power of a touch, a smile, a kind word, a listening ear, an honest compliment, or the smallest act of caring, all of which have the potential to turn a life around." - Leo Buscaglia

19. "Love is a fruit in season at all times, and within reach of every hand." - Mother Teresa

20. "Kindness begins with the understanding that we all struggle." - Charles Glassman

21. "Remember there's no such thing as a small act of kindness. Every act creates a ripple with no logical end." - Scott Adams

22. "The language of kindness is the lodestone of hearts and the spring of motives." - Lao Tzu

23. "We are made kind by being kind." - Eric Hoffer

24. "Act with kindness, but do not expect gratitude." - Confucius

25. "No act of kindness, no matter how small, is ever wasted." - Aesop

26. "Love is, above all, the gift of oneself." - Jean Anouilh

27. "The simplest acts of kindness are by far more powerful than a thousand heads bowing in prayer." - Mahatma Gandhi

28. "Love is something more stern and splendid than mere kindness." - C.S. Lewis

29. "Kind words can be short and easy to speak, but their echoes are truly endless." - Mother Teresa

30. "Love does not dominate; it cultivates." - Johann Wolfgang von Goethe

31. "One of the most spiritual things you can do is embrace your humanity. Connect with those around you today. Say 'I love you', 'I'm sorry', 'I appreciate you', 'I'm proud of you'... whatever you're feeling. Send random texts, write a cute note, embrace your truth and share it... cause a smile today for someone else... and give plenty of hugs." - Steve Maraboli

32. "Kindness and love are the essence of our humanity and are what connect us to the wider universe." - Unknown

33. "A part of kindness consists in loving people more than they deserve." - Joseph Joubert

34. "When you love someone, you love the person as they are, and not as you'd like them to be." - Leo Tolstoy

35. "Love cures people-both the ones who give it and the ones who receive it." - Karl Menninger

36. "In a world where you can be anything, be kind." - Jennifer Dukes Lee

37. "Treat everyone with politeness and kindness, not because they are nice, but because you are." - Roy T. Bennett

38. "Real kindness seeks no return; What return can the world make to rain clouds?" - Tiruvalluvar

39. "Three things in human life are important: the first is to be kind; the second is to be kind; and the third is to be kind." - Henry James

40. "One who knows how to show and to accept kindness will be a friend better than any possession." - Sophocles

41. "Kindness in ourselves is the honey that blunts the sting of unkindness in another." - Grantland Rice

42. "Love recognizes no barriers. It jumps hurdles, leaps fences, penetrates walls to arrive at its destination full of hope." - Maya Angelou

43. "Love is an act of endless forgiveness, a tender look which becomes a habit." - Peter Ustinov

44. "A random act of kindness, no matter how small, can make a tremendous impact on someone else's life." - Roy T. Bennett

45. "Only those who have learned the power of sincere and selfless contribution experience

life's deepest joy: true fulfillment." - Tony Robbins

46. "Love only grows by sharing. You can only have more for yourself by giving it away to others." - Brian Tracy

47. "When you are kind to others, it not only changes you, it changes the world." - Harold Kushner

48. "The best way to find yourself is to lose yourself in the service of others." - Mahatma Gandhi

49. "The smallest act of kindness is worth more than the grandest intention." - Oscar Wilde

50. "Love is not a mere sentiment or emotion; it is the ultimate truth at the heart of creation." - Rabindranath Tagore

51. "Love and kindness go hand in hand." - Marian Keyes

52. "You can't live a perfect day without doing something for someone who will never be able to repay you." - John Wooden

53. "Kindness is choosing love over hate, light over darkness, compassion over judgment." - Unknown

54. "We can't help everyone, but everyone can help someone." - Ronald Reagan

55. "Always find opportunities to make someone smile, and to offer random acts of kindness in everyday life." - Roy T. Bennett

56. "Kindness is more important than wisdom, and the recognition of this is the beginning of wisdom." - Theodore Isaac Rubin

57. "Love is not patronizing and charity isn't about pity, it is about love. Charity and love are the same-with charity you give love, so don't just give money but reach out your hand instead." - Mother Teresa

58. "If you judge people, you have no time to love them." - Mother Teresa

59. "Life becomes easier and more beautiful when we can see the good in other people." - Roy T. Bennett

60.   "Be kind whenever possible. It is always possible." - Dalai Lama

PART 3:

FORGIVENESS AND HEALING

Quotes on the power of forgiveness and moving past hurt.

1. "Forgiveness does not change the past, but it does enlarge the future." - Paul Boese

2. "The weak can never forgive. Forgiveness is the attribute of the strong." - Mahatma Gandhi

3. "To forgive is to set a prisoner free and discover that the prisoner was you." - Lewis B. Smedes

4. "Forgiveness is not an occasional act, it is a constant attitude." - Martin Luther King Jr.

5. "Forgiveness is the fragrance that the violet sheds on the heel that has crushed it." - Mark Twain

6. "Forgiveness says you are given another chance to make a new beginning." - Desmond Tutu

7. "The act of forgiveness takes place in our own mind. It really has nothing to do with the other person." - Louise Hay

8. "Forgiveness is the key to action and freedom." - Hannah Arendt

9. "To err is human; to forgive, divine." - Alexander Pope

10. "Resentment is like drinking poison and then hoping it will kill your enemies." - Nelson Mandela

11. "Forgiveness liberates the soul. It removes fear. That is why it is such a powerful weapon." - Nelson Mandela

12. "Forgiveness is the giving, and so the receiving, of life." - George MacDonald

13. "Forgiveness isn't just the absence of anger. I think it's also the presence of self-love, when you actually begin to value yourself." - Tara Westover

14. "Forgiveness is the final form of love." - Reinhold Niebuhr

15. "It's one of the greatest gifts you can give yourself, to forgive. Forgive everybody." - Maya Angelou

16. "Forgiveness is a virtue of the brave." - Indira Gandhi

17. "When you forgive, you in no way change the past - but you sure do change the future." - Bernard Meltzer

18. "Forgiveness is a reflection of loving yourself enough to move on." - Dr. Steve Maraboli

19. "Letting go doesn't mean that you don't care about someone anymore. It's just realizing that the only person you really have control over is yourself." - Deborah Reber

20. "The practice of forgiveness is our most important contribution to the healing of the world." - Marianne Williamson

21. "Without forgiveness, life is governed by... an endless cycle of resentment and retaliation." - Roberto Assagioli

22. "The first to apologize is the bravest. The first to forgive is the strongest. The first to forget is the happiest." - Unknown

23. "Not forgiving is like drinking rat poison and then waiting for the rat to die." - Anne Lamott

24. "You can't let your failures define you. You have to let your failures teach you." - Barack Obama

25. "Forgiving what we cannot forgive creates a new way to remember. We change the memory of our past into a hope for our future." - Lewis Smedes

26. "Forgiveness is choosing to love. It is the first skill of self-giving love." - Mahatma Gandhi

27. "Let us forgive each other - only then will we live in peace." - Leo Tolstoy

28. "An eye for an eye, and the whole world would be blind." - Kahlil Gibran

29. "Forgiveness is the needle that knows how to mend." - Jewel

30. "Always forgive your enemies; nothing annoys them so much." - Oscar Wilde

31. "What is forgiven is usually well remembered." - Louis Dudek

32. "Holding onto anger is like grasping a hot coal with the intent of throwing it at someone else; you are the one who gets burned." - Buddha

33. "Forgive others, not because they deserve forgiveness, but because you deserve peace." - Jonathan Lockwood Huie

34. "There is no love without forgiveness, and there is no forgiveness without love." - Bryant H. McGill

35. "The art of forgiveness is the art of letting go. Once you do that, you can really move on." - Zoe Kravitz

36. "In the blink of an eye, everything can change. So forgive often and love with all your heart. You may never know when you may not have that chance again." - Unknown

37. "Forgiveness is not about forgetting. It is about letting go of another person's throat." - William Paul Young

38. "Forgiveness is the process of dropping off your emotional baggage." - Tim Fargo

39. "Grudges are for those who insist that they are owed something; forgiveness, however, is for those who are substantial enough to move on." - Criss Jami

40. "The heart of a mother is a deep abyss at the bottom of which you will always find forgiveness." - Honoré de Balzac

41. "When a deep injury is done to us, we never heal until we forgive." - Nelson Mandela

42. "The stupid neither forgive nor forget; the naive forgive and forget; the wise forgive but do not forget." - Thomas Szasz

43. "Only the brave know how to forgive... a coward never forgave; it is not in his nature." - Laurence Sterne

44. "Forgiveness is a sign that the person who has wronged you means more to you than the wrong they have dealt." - Ben Greenhalgh

45. "Forgiveness is the sweetest revenge." - Isaac Friedmann

46. "Forgiveness is the key that unlocks the door of resentment and the handcuffs of hatred. It is a power that breaks the chains of bitterness and the shackles of selfishness." - Corrie ten Boom

47. "Forgiveness is the only way to dissolve that link and get free." - Catherine Ponder

48. "Forgiveness means giving up all hope for a better past." - Lily Tomlin

49. "There is a nobility in compassion, a beauty in empathy, a grace in forgiveness." - John Connolly

50. "Life becomes easier when you learn to accept an apology you never got." - Robert Brault

51. "Forgiveness isn't approving what happened. It's choosing to rise above it." - Robin Sharma

52. "True forgiveness is when you can say, 'Thank you for that experience.'" - Oprah Winfrey

53. "Forgiving you is my gift to you. Moving on is my gift to myself." - Unknown

54. "There is no revenge so complete as forgiveness." - Josh Billings

55. "To be wronged is nothing unless you continue to remember it." - Confucius

CHAPTER 4:

QUOTES ON MINDFULNESS AND INNER PEACE

PART 1:

BEING PRESENT

Quotes about the importance of living in the moment.

1. "Be happy in the moment, that's enough. Each moment is all we need, not more." - Mother Teresa

2. "The ability to be in the present moment is a major component of mental wellness." - Abraham Maslow

3. "Life is available only in the present moment." - Thich Nhat Hanh

4. "The point of power is always in the present moment." - Louise Hay

5. "Wherever you are, be all there." - Jim Elliot

6. "Realize deeply that the present moment is all you have. Make the NOW the primary focus of your life." - Eckhart Tolle

7. "Yesterday is history, tomorrow is a mystery, and today is a gift... that's why they call it present." - Master Oogway

8. "Being present means living without control and always having your needs met." - Marshall B. Rosenberg

9. "The best way to capture moments is to pay attention. This is how we cultivate mindfulness." - Jon Kabat-Zinn

10. "If you want to conquer the anxiety of life, live in the moment, live in the breath." - Amit Ray

11. "Be present in all things and thankful for all things." - Maya Angelou

12. "Living in the moment means letting go of the past and not waiting for the future. It means living your life consciously, aware that each moment you breathe is a gift." - Oprah Winfrey

13. "Forever is composed of nows." - Emily Dickinson

14. "You must live in the present, launch yourself on every wave, find your eternity in each moment." - Henry David Thoreau

15. "The present moment is filled with joy and happiness. If you are attentive, you will see it." - Thich Nhat Hanh

16. "Do not dwell in the past, do not dream of the future, concentrate the mind on the present moment." - Buddha

17. "In the midst of movement and chaos, keep stillness inside of you." - Deepak Chopra

18. "Mindfulness means being awake. It means knowing what you are doing." - Jon Kabat-Zinn

19. "Breathe and let be." - Jon Kabat-Zinn

20. "This is real freedom-the ability to enjoy the choices we make in every successive moment of the present." - Deepak Chopra

21. "The secret of health for both mind and body is not to mourn for the past, not to worry about the future, but to live the present moment wisely and earnestly." - Buddha

22. "Mindfulness isn't difficult, we just need to remember to do it." - Sharon Salzberg

23. "The only way to live is by accepting each minute as an unrepeatable miracle." - Tara Brach

24. "One today is worth two tomorrows." - Benjamin Franklin

25. "Be present-it is the only moment that matters." - Dan Millman

26. "Now is the only time. How we relate to it creates the future. What we do accumulates; the future is the result of what we do right now." - Pema Chödrön

27. "Each moment is a place you've never been." - Mark Strand

28. "It stands to reason that anyone who learns to live well will die well. The skills are the same: being present in the moment, and humble, and brave, and keeping a sense of humor." - Victoria Moran

29. "The art of life is to live in the present moment." - Emmet Fox

30. "The here and now is all we have, and if we play it right it's all we'll need." - Ann Richards

31. "When you are present, you can allow the mind to be as it is without getting entangled in it." - Eckhart Tolle

32. "A great place to start is where you are." - Jean Borysenko

33. "To live in the present moment is a miracle." - Thich Nhat Hanh

34. "The present moment, if you think about it, is the only time there is. No matter what time it is, it is always now." - Marianne Williamson

35. "Present-moment living, getting in touch with your now, is at the heart of effective living." - Wayne Dyer

36. "The aim of life is to live, and to live means to be aware, joyously, drunkenly, serenely, divinely aware." - Henry Miller

37. "When you try to control everything, you enjoy nothing. Relax, breathe, let go, and just live." - Unknown

38. "Live in the present and make it so beautiful that it will be worth remembering." - Ida Scott Taylor

39. "Practice the art of living in the present moment." - Melody Beattie

40. "Stop acting as if life is a rehearsal. Live this day as if it were your last. The past is over and gone. The future is not guaranteed." - Wayne Dyer

41. "Yesterday's the past, tomorrow's the future, but today is a gift. That's why it's called the present." - Bil Keane

42. "Don't let the past steal your present." - Terri Guillemets

43. "With mindfulness, you can establish yourself in the present in order to touch the wonders of life that are available in that moment." - Thich Nhat Hanh

44. "Life can only be understood backwards; but it must be lived forwards." - Søren Kierkegaard

45. "Living in the present moment creates the experience of eternity." - Deepak Chopra

46. "Being present is being connected to All Things." - S. Kelley Harrell

47. "The present is never our end. The past and present are our means; the future alone is our end." - Blaise Pascal

48. "The gift of the present is the only gift that is real." - Eckhart Tolle

49. "Presence is more than just being there." - Malcolm Forbes

50. "Whatever the present moment contains, accept it as if you had chosen it." - Eckhart Tolle

51. "Worry never robs tomorrow of its sorrow, it only saps today of its joy." - Leo F. Buscaglia

52. "There is only one time that is important-Now! It is the most important time because it is the only time when we have any power." - Leo Tolstoy

53. "The past is a ghost, the future a dream. All we ever have is now." - Bill Cosby

54.   "The present is the ever-moving shadow that divides yesterday from tomorrow. In that lies hope." - Frank Lloyd Wright

PART 2:

MEDITATION AND REFLECTION

Sayings that encourage reflection and internal peace.

1. "Meditation is the soul's perspective glass." - Owen Feltham

2. "Reflection is the lamp of the heart. If it departs, the heart will have no light." - Imam Al-Haddad

3. "Meditation is not a way of making your mind quiet. It is a way of entering into the quiet that is already there – buried under the 50,000 thoughts the average person thinks every day." - Deepak Chopra

4. "The soul usually knows what to do to heal itself. The challenge is to silence the mind." - Caroline Myss

5. "Meditation and concentration are the way to a life of serenity." - Baba Ram Dass

6. "We cannot see our reflection in running water. It is only in still water that we can see." - Zen Proverb

7. "Your calm mind is the ultimate weapon against your challenges. So relax." - Bryant McGill

8. "Reflection is one of the most underused yet powerful tools for success." - Richard Carlson

9. "Self-reflection is the school of wisdom." - Baltasar Gracian

10. "Meditation is like a gym in which you develop the powerful mental muscles of calm and insight." - Ajahn Brahm

11. "By the practice of meditation, you will find that you are carrying within your heart a portable paradise." - Paramahansa Yogananda

12. "Reflection on the infinite seems to call, almost by definition, for infinite reflection." - Daniel Taylor

13. "Through my love for you, I want to express my love for the whole cosmos, the whole of humanity, and all beings. By living with you, I want to learn to love everyone and all species." - Thich Nhat Hanh

14. "Quiet the mind, and the soul will speak." - Ma Jaya Sati Bhagavati

15. "Without reflection, we go blindly on our way, creating more unintended consequences, and failing to achieve anything useful." - Margaret J. Wheatley

16. "Meditation is the dissolution of thoughts in Eternal awareness or Pure consciousness without objectification, knowing without thinking, merging finitude in infinity." - Swami Sivananda

17. "He who reflects more than others will become wiser than others." - Denis Diderot

18. "To understand the immeasurable, the mind must be extraordinarily quiet, still." - Jiddu Krishnamurti

19. "The more tranquil a man becomes, the greater is his success, his influence, his power for good." - James Allen

20. "The reflection of the world is blues, that's where that part of the music is at. Then you got this other kind of music that's tryin' to come around." - Jimi Hendrix

21. "In the attitude of silence the soul finds the path in a clearer light, and what is elusive and deceptive resolves itself into crystal clearness." - Mahatma Gandhi

22. "Meditation can help us embrace our worries, our fear, our anger; and that is very healing. We let our own natural capacity of healing do the work." - Thich Nhat Hanh

23. "The greatest journey is the journey inwards. Of him who has chosen his destiny, Who has started upon his quest for the source of his being." - Dag Hammarskjöld

24. "Meditation is not evasion; it is a serene encounter with reality." - Thich Nhat Hanh

25. "Spend some time alone every day." - Dalai Lama

26. "An unreflected life is not worth living." - Socrates

27. "Meditation is the tongue of the soul and the language of our spirit." - Jeremy Taylor

28. "What lies behind us and what lies before us are tiny matters compared to what lies within us." - Ralph Waldo Emerson

29. "Everything that irritates us about others can lead us to an understanding of ourselves." - Carl Jung

30. "Knowing yourself is the beginning of all wisdom." - Aristotle

31. "Inner peace begins the moment you choose not to allow another person or event to control your emotions." - Pema Chödrön

32. "You should sit in meditation for twenty minutes every day - unless you're too busy. Then you should sit for an hour." - Zen proverb

33. "If you want to find God, hang out in the space between your thoughts." - Alan Cohen

34. "The heart of meditation is taking ourselves a little less seriously." - Ethan Nichtern

35. "In the light of calm and steady self-awareness, inner energies wake up and work miracles without any effort on your part." - Nisargadatta Maharaj

36. "Prayer is when you talk to God; meditation is when you listen to God." - Diana Robinson

37. "Every moment and every event of every man's life on earth plants something in his soul." - Thomas Merton

38. "The thing about meditation is: you become more and more you." - David Lynch

39. "When there are thoughts, it is distraction: when there are no thoughts, it is meditation." - Ramana Maharshi

40. "Wisdom comes with the ability to be still. Just look and just listen. No more is needed." - Eckhart Tolle

41. "Meditation is the discovery that the point of life is always arrived at in the immediate moment." - Alan Watts

42. "Adopt the pace of nature: her secret is patience." - Ralph Waldo Emerson

43. "Meditation is not a means to an end. It is both the means and the end." - Jiddu Krishnamurti

44. "Only in quiet waters do things mirror themselves undistorted. Only in a quiet mind is adequate perception of the world." - Hans Margolius

45. "Meditation is a way for nourishing and blossoming the divinity within you." - Amit Ray

46. "The thing about meditation is you become more and more you." - David Lynch

47. "Silence is a source of great strength." - Lao Tzu

48. "Meditation brings wisdom; lack of meditation leaves ignorance." - Buddha

49. "To a mind that is still, the whole universe surrenders." - Lao Tzu

50. "Reflection allows you to ponder on the deeper meaning of the experiences in your life." - Unknown

51. "Meditation is the ultimate mobile device; you can use it anywhere, anytime, unobtrusively." - Sharon Salzberg

52. "Reflection is not the evil; but a reflective condition and the deadlock which it involves, by transforming the capacity to act into a means of escape from action." - Søren Kierkegaard

53. "Mindfulness is about being fully awake in our lives. It is about perceiving the exquisite vividness of each moment." - Jon Kabat-Zinn

54. "Meditate. Live purely. Be quiet. Do your work with mastery. Like the moon, come out from behind the clouds! Shine." - Buddha

55. "Reflection is the business of man." - Samuel Johnson

56. "Meditation is the art of cleaning your mirror from time to time." - Rajneesh

57. "True reflection comes when you can sit quietly and listen to the story that your soul wants to tell you." - Unknown

PART 3:

SPIRITUAL WISDOM

Quotes that offer spiritual insights and
enlightenment.

1. "The only true wisdom is in knowing you know nothing." - Socrates

2. "Knowing others is wisdom, knowing yourself is Enlightenment." - Lao Tzu

3. "The way to do is to be." - Lao Tzu

4. "As you start to walk on the way, the way appears." - Rumi

5. "Spiritual progress is like a detoxification." - Marianne Williamson

6. "You have to grow from the inside out. None can teach you, none can make you spiritual. There is no other teacher but your own soul." - Swami Vivekananda

7. "The privilege of a lifetime is to become who you truly are." - Carl Jung

8. "We are not human beings having a spiritual experience. We are spiritual beings having a human experience." - Pierre Teilhard de Chardin

9. "All major religious traditions carry basically the same message, that is love, compassion and forgiveness the important thing is they should be part of our daily lives." - Dalai Lama

10. "What you are is God's gift to you, what you become is your gift to God." - Hans Urs von Balthasar

11. "When you connect to the silence within you, that is when you can make sense of the disturbance going on around you." - Stephen Richards

12. "To understand everything is to forgive everything." - Buddha

13. "Beyond the ideas of wrongdoing and rightdoing, there is a field. I'll meet you there." - Rumi

14. "The soul would have no rainbow if the eyes had no tears." - Native American Proverb

15. "Spirituality does not come from religion. It comes from our soul." - Anthony Douglas Williams

16. "Your sacred space is where you can find yourself again and again." - Joseph Campbell

17. "He who knows others is wise; he who knows himself is enlightened." - Lao Tzu

18. "People only see what they are prepared to see." - Ralph Waldo Emerson

19. "Awakening is not changing who you are, but discarding who you are not." - Deepak Chopra

20. "The real spiritual progress of the aspirant is measured by the extent to which he achieves inner tranquility." - Swami Sivananda

21. "Do not follow the ideas of others, but learn to listen to the voice within yourself." - Zen Master Dogen

22. "Enlightenment is when a wave realizes it is the ocean." - Thich Nhat Hanh

23. "Faith is the bird that feels the light when the dawn is still dark." - Rabindranath Tagore

24. "The quieter you become, the more you can hear." - Baba Ram Dass

25. "Seek not to follow in the footsteps of the wise. Seek what they sought." - Matsuo Basho

26. "There are many paths to enlightenment. Be sure to take one with a heart." - Lao Tzu

27. "The kingdom of heaven is within you; and whosoever shall know himself shall find it." - Ancient Egyptian Proverb

28. "Spirituality is recognizing and celebrating that we are all inextricably connected to each other by a power greater than all of us, and that our

connection to that power and to one another is grounded in love and compassion." - Brené Brown

29. "Prayer is the key of the morning and the bolt of the evening." - Mahatma Gandhi

30. "Everything that is made beautiful and fair and lovely is made for the eye of one who sees." - Rumi

31. "The greatest illusion in this world is the illusion of separation." - Unknown

32. "Spirituality is not to be learned by flight from the world, or by running away from things, or by turning solitary and going apart from the world. Rather, we must learn an inner solitude wherever or with whomever we are. We must learn to penetrate things and find God there." - Meister Eckhart

33. "Your task is not to seek for love, but merely to seek and find all the barriers within yourself that you have built against it." - Rumi

34. "At the core of your heart, you are perfect and pure. No one and nothing can alter that." - Amit Ray

35. "Do not let the behavior of others destroy your inner peace." - Dalai Lama

36. "The wound is the place where the Light enters you." - Rumi

37. "The most beautiful experience we can have is the mysterious." - Albert Einstein

38. "Everything in the universe is within you. Ask all from yourself." - Rumi

39. "God resides in the heart of every human being." - Indian Proverb

40. "A quiet mind is able to hear intuition over fear." - Yvan Byeajee

41. "The way to love anything is to realize that it may be lost." - Gilbert K. Chesterton

42. "Let your faith be bigger than your fears, have faith success will be near." - Unknown

43. "I searched for God and found only myself. I searched for myself and found only God." - Sufi Proverb

44. "Believe in your infinite potential. Your only limitations are those you set upon yourself." - Roy T. Bennett

45. "The more light you allow within you, the brighter the world you live in will be." - Shakti Gawain

46. "Silence is sometimes the best answer." - Dalai Lama

47. "The only real valuable thing is intuition." - Albert Einstein

48. "The most authentic thing about us is our capacity to create, to overcome, to endure, to transform, to love, and to be greater than our suffering." - Ben Okri

49. "When the ego dies, the soul awakes." - Mahatma Gandhi

50. "The spiritual life does not remove us from the world but leads us deeper into it." - Henri J.M. Nouwen

51. "Each person comes into this world with a specific destiny-he has something to fulfill, some message has to be delivered, some work has to be completed. You are not here accidentally-you are here meaningfully. There is a purpose behind you. The whole intends to do something through you." - Osho

52. "A mind that is stretched by a new experience can never go back to its old dimensions." - Oliver Wendell Holmes, Jr.

53. "There are things known and there are things unknown, and in between are the doors of perception." - Aldous Huxley

I hope you have enjoyed this timeless wisdom left by the greatest minds of all time. I wish that they will help you achieve a happy, uplifting and successful life.

I believe you deserve to be happy and to achieve all of your dreams. You are on the right path, never give up!

Good luck on your journey my friend!

ABOUT THE AUTHOR

I remember it like I was yesterday. I was 7, living with my grandmother in the countryside in a little town of only 800 people, when my parents came and took me away on the greatest journey of my life. Living on 3 continents and in 5 countries, little did I know where life would take me decades later. Halfway across the word. Despite a lifetime of tirelessly educating myself and working in Private Equity in one of the most revered financial capitals of the world, little did I know that I would end up reaching the age of 37 having to begin all over again.

Finally learning that a life long of learning has just begun.
Humbled by the realization that I actually know very little.

Life is like that, one day you feel like you are on top of the world and the next you realize you have a lot to learn. Through the good times and the bad, I have learned that staying resilient and motivated is one of the most important things and there is no better way than learning from amazing people and through beautiful experiences. What more amazing people could we wish to learn from then from the greatest minds of all time who have changed the world as we know it and have blessed us with their teachings. Which they have generously left in their numerous texts. Gold mines scattered through history waiting for us to discover them.

These important lessons have changed the course of millions before us and they are now here to light out path to success.

Good luck on your journey dear friends, may you gain the success you seek and the happiness you deserve.

Daniel Bulmez

Made in United States
Troutdale, OR
11/05/2024

24431465R00066